100 Historic American Flags

By

John Caskey

Contents

≈

Introduction

For over 3,000 years, flags have captured the imaginations of the people of planet Earth and have figured prominently in their battles, ceremonies, religious affairs, parades, pageantry and affiliations. Flags as we know them today were *almost* certainly the original inspiration of the ancient Chinese in the 2nd Millennium B.C.E., with the proviso being that the ancient Indian cultures may have unfurled their first flags concurrent with—or possibly even before—the ancient Chinese flag pioneers of the Chou Dynasty.

We know from Chinese history that the respectful identification of a flag with the very object it represents (leader, military unit, or country) was a part of flag decorum from the very start. In ancient China, the emperor's flag was the personification of the leader himself. It was as serious a crime to touch the emperor's flag uninvited as it was to touch the emperor's person, and for a military leader's flag to fall in battle surely indicated defeat to the point of scattering an army. Today, flag bearers of military units are still typically individuals of outstanding reputation in their units, and national flags are associated with elaborate codes of protocol and respectful display. It is still not unusual for disrespectful treatment of a national flag to carry with it serious criminal penalties, the freedom of symbolic speech notwithstanding.

It is not completely settled from what original source the use of flags entered Western Europe and subsequently was adopted in the United States. The ancient Romans typically carried sacred symbols and effigies of various gods atop staffs into battle, and in time these objects were standardized by the well-known Roman Eagle. By the First Century C.E. we know from the historian Livy that at least some Roman cavalry units were carrying a "vexillum", or small cloth banner affixed to a *horizontal* staff atop a pole. In the 4th Century C.E. the Emperor

1

Constantine the Great standardized the vexillum with the Chi Rho insignia of his "labarum" for Byzantine military units, and the Orthodox Christian Church adopted processional "labara" used to this day.

However, historians think that it was the crusades and the flags of the Islamic armies and navies that captured the imaginations of Western Europe. Islamic groups adopted Indian flag practices with their expansion into Southern Asia, but Islamic religious practices frowned on even symbolic representations placed on flags. Accordingly, the original Islamic armies in Western Asia and Southern Europe displayed large flowing flags of solid colors with various colors representing different dynasties. The original flag of Mohammed's armies was black, but in time red, white and green flags were utilized.

The crusaders returning to Northern Europe brought with them flag customs of the Islamic armies, but in time they made their own contributions to flag history. A *standard* became the flag of the monarch and specified military positions such as a castle or ship. *Banners* were flags borne into battle by military groups headed by royalty and the greater nobility, often displaying the leader's coat of arms. The *guidon* was a smaller flag permitted to knights and their groups, often with swallow tails or rounded fly ends. The *pennon* was a small triangular flag carried by individual knights on the business end of their lances both as a safety measure and also as an intimidation display to the enemy. Medieval sailing ships adopted elegant tapering *pennants*, some measuring nearly 100 feet long, to hoist from their masts at sea. These maritime pennants became, in time, limited to royal or national naval (military) vessels, the forerunners of the modern *ensigns*. Originally ensigns were the personal flags of the highest ranking officer aboard a vessel, but in time they became the maritime flag of the nation-state that operated the vessel. The maritime equivalent of banners and guidons used aboard vessels became the *jacks* of modern usage displayed on the jack staff at the front of a vessel.

Flag terminology can be complicated and a bit tricky depending upon the context of use of a particular flag. The part of a flag nearest the pole is referred to as the *hoist*. The measurement of the hoist is the flag's *width*. The outer edge of the flag, as well as the distance between the hoist and the outer edge, is called the *fly*. The upper hoist quadrant (usually but not always) of the flag is called the *canton*, and the background color of the flag exclusive of the canton or an ornament (or "badge") is called the flag's *field*. Recall the name of the first Roman flag, the "vexillum." The study of flags is called "vexillology", and a flag expert is a "vexillologist".

American Flag Design

By resolution dated June 14, 1777 (traditionally, "Flag Day" in the United States), the Marine Committee of the Second Continental Congress declared simply:

"Resolved, that the flag of the United States be thirteen stripes, alternate red and white; that the union [canton] be thirteen stars, white in a blue field representing a new constellation."

The flag with a circle of thirteen stars on a blue field and thirteen stripes appeared soon thereafter and was even painted in anachronistically on paintings depicting earlier events. Until the Flag Act of 1794 this flag was (correctly so) referred to as the Naval Ensign of the United States. General George Washington, as was his prerogative, adopted his own flag design for the Continental Army, the so-called "Great Union Flag." However Congress never formally adopted the Great Union Flag for the Army of the United States. By default, the Naval Ensign became the national flag of the United States by custom by 1781.

With the Flag Act of 1794, and to reflect the entry of Vermont (1791) and Kentucky (1792) into the Union, the number of stripes of the original national flag of the United States (June 14, 1777) was increased from 13 to 15, and the field of stars was increased as well in the canton. This famous fifteen stripes, fifteen stars flag, popularly known as the "Star Spangled Banner", was the United States Flag during the War of 1812.

From the Flag Act of 1794 until April 4, 1818 the flag was not *officially* changed at all despite the entry of five new states into the Union on the historical assumption that adding new stripes and new stars with each new state's admission would create visual clutter. On April 4, 1818, Congress addressed the United States Flag for the first time in a quarter century, and at the suggestion of a naval captain directed that the number of stars in the Flag reflect the number of states in the Union, but the stripes be permanently reduced from fifteen to thirteen in honor of the original 13 colonies of the United States. Moreover, the new directions dictated that new State additions of any future year would become effective on July 4th following entry of a new state into the Union. By law (actually the omission of any law to the contrary), all of the previous flag designs of the United States are still "official flags" of the country and may be flown and honored with the same dignity accorded the most current version of the flag.

Today, the United States Code specifies only the following as to the design of the Nation's flag:

"The flag of the United States shall be thirteen horizontal stripes, alternate red and white; and the union of the flag shall be forty-eight stars [at the time of the last passage of the Act], white in a blue field." 4 U.S.C. Section 1

"On the admission of a new State into the Union one star shall be added to the union of the flag; and such addition shall

4

take effect on the fourth day of July then next succeeding such admission." 4 U.S.C. Section 2

As was the case with the June 14, 1777 original resolution of the Marine Committee of the Second Continental Congress, no *law* mandates a specific arrangement of the stars of the American Flag, leaving open various designs that were popular in the 19th Century as alternates to a rectangular pattern. Nothing prohibits alternative star arrangements on the American Flag's blue canton, as long as flag respect and decorum is maintained (Section 8 of the Flag Code).

4 U.S.C. Section 10, however, specifies that: *"Any rule or custom pertaining to the display of the flag of the United States of America, set forth herein, may be altered, modified, or repealed, or additional rules with respect thereto may be prescribed, by the Commander in Chief of the Armed Forces of the United States, whenever he deems it to be appropriate or desirable; and any such alteration or additional rule shall be set forth in a proclamation."*

Utilizing Section 10 of the Flag Code, a Presidential Proclamation issued in the Eisenhower Administration (see below) has now standardized American Flag colors, dimensions and proportions *for purposes of American Flags used by the Federal Government only*. Private citizens, companies, and the various States of the Union may make American Flags as they see fit, governed only by Sections 1 & 2 of the Flag Code and (as always) the respect and decorum requirements of Section 8. Therefore, it is not unusual to see American Flags flying with slightly different color shades and different proportions than the Federal Flags.

American Flag Etiquette

The Federal Flag Code, first adopted by the United States in 1942, is formally set forth in Title 4 of the United States Code, Sections 4-10, and is intended as a *guideline* for United States civilians without penalties for non-compliance. Section 5. It is expected that patriotic Americans will follow the Flag Code without compulsion. The general rule of the Flag Code is that "[n]o disrespect should be shown to the flag of the United States of America" [4 U.S.C. 8], and so actions and practical flag display situations not covered by the Code (and there are many) are left to the sound discretion of the American handling the flag as long as his or her actions are in conformity with the general rule of respect.

Attempts at proscribing criminal penalties for intentional disrespect to the American Flag have been repeatedly overruled by the United States Supreme Court based on that Court's interpretation of constitutionally permissible "symbolic speech." As much as Americans may disagree with that Court's constitutional position, such seems to be the present law of the land, notwithstanding State Laws such as Washington's RC 9.86.020 & 9.86.030 and Idaho's 18-3401 making it a misdemeanor to "cast contempt upon" or "publicly mutilate . . ." a flag of the United States or of the State.

Section 4 of the Flag Code adopts by law the *Pledge of Allegiance* to the Flag, and states that the pledge should be made while standing at attention facing the flag with the right hand over the heart. Only men in uniform may say the pledge with their uniform hats on, as men not in uniform must remove any headdress not required to remain on by religious conscious with their right hand and place the hat with their right hand on their left shoulder while their hand is held over their heart during the recitation of the Pledge. Section 4 does not address women and hats, but implied is the long standing American custom that

6

women need not remove their hats. Persons in uniform should render their military salute and may remain silent. Veterans of the United States military and members of the military not in uniform may nevertheless salute, at their option. All branches of Boy Scouts and Girl Scouts in uniform may give their official salute.

Section 6 of the Flag Code sets forth the proper *time* to display the American Flag. The Flag is customarily displayed only from dawn to dusk, but if properly illuminated may be flown during nighttime hours as well. It is not customary to fly the Flag in inclement weather unless it is of an all weather design. The Flag ought to be flown on all National and State holidays, including, of course, Flag Day (June 14). Public institutions (State and Federal), polling places, and schools ought display the Flag on every day these places are open for business, voting or education.

Section 6 of the Flag Code also directs that the American Flag be "hoisted briskly and lowered ceremoniously". During raising and lowering, the same provisions apply for military and non-military persons as do during the Pledge of Allegiance. Section 9. Additionally, however, while non-citizens are not required to recite the Pledge of Allegiance, they are nevertheless instructed to stand at attention when the American Flag is raised and lowered. Likewise, when watching a parade in which the American Flag is carried, it is customary to stand at attention when the Flag passes.

Section 7 is the longest and most detailed provision of the Flag Code and addresses decorum and protocol in *displaying* the American Flag. There are many do's and don'ts in Section 7, but the basic principles of flag display are consistent and easy to remember. First, with the sole exception of it being permissible to drape an American Flag over a coffin of a deceased American Veteran, the Flag must always be displayed from a staff or flag pole when not displayed on a wall with the canton (the Stars on a background of blue) positioned to the Flag's own right.

When draped over a coffin, the flag is positioned with the canton of stars placed toward the head of the decedent and over the left breast. Positionally, the *usual rule* is that the American Flag is always placed to *its own right* of any other flag, slightly ahead and at a higher position than any flags displayed with the American Flag, and at the forward center in a line or procession of other flags.

Prior to the American Bicentennial in 1976, a complicated rule of flag etiquette stated that when the audience of an event was on the same level as the American Flag on display (as opposed to the Flag being situated on an elevated stage or platform), then in that event the American Flag was positioned to the audience's right. However, there was much confusion as to when this rule applied and under what special circumstances, and recent amendments to the Flag Code have omitted this arcane rule. Now we are safe in assuming that the American Flag is *always* placed to the audience's left (speaker's right) however situated and usually alone – with all other flags placed on the other side of the speaker.

There are special provisions applicable for United States naval vessels and the flags of the United Nations at that organization's headquarters in New York City. When other flags are flown with the American Flag, the American Flag must be positioned in a superior place on the pole, and in a line of outdoor flags the American Flag must always be raised first and lowered last. International Law forbids any flag of one nation to be positioned higher than the flag of another *in time of peace*. When displayed on a cable over a street, the Flag's canton must always be positioned to the north in an east-west street and to the east in a north-south street. In an auditorium, a wall mounted Flag must be placed in a raised position behind the speaker's podium. The same directional positioning applies when the Flag is suspended in corridor or lobby of a building.

As previously stated, Section 8 of the Flag Code sets forth the general position that the American Flag must always be displayed and carried *with respect*. The American Flag ought not be dipped when carried in deference to any other flag. The Flag ought not be allowed to touch the ground or any fixed object when carried, displayed or when raising or lowering. The Flag's canton must always be displayed upward, with the only exception being when the Flag is used as a recognized distress signal with the canton displayed downward.

The Flag ought not be carried or displayed flat or horizontally, even though very large flags displayed in athletic events are sometimes displayed this way due to the impracticability of displaying such large flags from a pole or staff. The Flag must never be used as clothing, bedding, drapery, or modified or defaced in any manner. The Flag ought not be used in advertizing, nor printed on disposable items such as paper plates and napkins. A Flag lapel pin ought be worn on the left lapel.

Section 8 of the Flag Code concludes with the advice that "[t]he flag, when it is in such condition that it is no longer a fitting emblem for display, should be destroyed in a dignified way, preferably by burning." Flags may certainly be washed, cleaned and repaired when possible. It is the current custom in the United States *not* to burn Flags made of synthetic materials in solemn Flag Retirement Ceremonies for pollution and fire safety reasons. Such Flags may, however, be buried when rendered unserviceable.

A separate law, the Freedom to Display the American Flag Act (2005), prohibits real estate covenants or restrictions on the display of the American Flag by homeowners.

There are special provisions for when the American Flag is flown at half-mast. When this is appropriate, the Flag must be raised completely to the top of a pole or staff and then lowered to the half-mast position. When taken down, the Flag must be again raised to the top of the pole or staff and lowered. On Memorial Day the Flag is flown at half-mast until noon only, and then raised to the top of the pole or staff for the remainder of the holiday.

Section 10 of the Flag Code allows the Code to be modified or added to by executive order of the President of the United States, and indeed during the administration of President Eisenhower (1952-1960) two such Presidential Orders were issued. Executive Order 3044 entered by President Dwight Eisenhower on March 1, 1954, directed that the American Flag be flown at half mast following the death: of any American President or former American President for 30 days following death; of the Vice-President, Chief Justice or retired Chief Justice, or Speaker of the House of Representatives for 10 days following death; of a former Vice-President, Associate Justice of the Supreme Court, Cabinet Member, President Pro Tempore of the Senate, Majority Leader of the Senate, Minority Leader of the Senate, Majority Leader of the House of Representatives, or Minority Leader of the House of Representatives from the day of death until internment; of a U.S. Senator, Representative, Territorial Delegate, or Resident Commissioner from the Commonwealth of Puerto Rico from the day of death until internment, in the District of Columbia and the jurisdictions which they died serving; and of all governors from the day of death until internment in their respective jurisdictions.

Executive Order 10834 entered by President Dwight Eisenhower on August 21, 1959, set forth specific colors and dimensions of the constituent parts of the flag, and authorized overall flag dimensions "for executive agencies [*i.e.,* of the Federal Government]". The Eisenhower Presidential Proclamations have now been incorporated into the Flag Code.

Flags of the Early Explorers & Settlers

 1 The expedition of Christopher Columbus to the "New World" and what would become America was with the official patronage of King Ferdinand and Queen Ysabel (or "Isabel") of the country we refer to as "Spain" today. Therefore, the Pinta, the Nina and the Santa Maria all flew **The Columbus Maritime Ensign** with a symbolic "F" and "Y" joined by a green cross on a field of white.

 2 Ferdinand was King of Aragon and Sicily. His wife Ysabel was Queen of Castile and Leon. In addition to the two sovereigns' ensign, the ships of the Columbus expedition *may have* carried **The Flag of Castile and Leon** (the Queen's Flag), although this specific flag is not mentioned in the Columbus log book.

 3 In addition to The Columbus Maritime Ensign, **The Royal Standard of the Catholic Kings** was *definitely* a flag carried by Columbus and explicitly referred to in his log book. In the October 12, 1492, log book entry by Columbus, he specifically stated that his crew carried both The Columbus Maritime Ensign and The Royal Standard ashore on San Salvador Island to claim the New World for Spain. The first and fourth quarters of the Royal Standard are the emblems of Castile and Leon in honor of the Spanish Queen, and the second and third quarters display the emblems of Aragon and Sicily in honor of the Spanish King.

4 Spain was the first European country to explore North America, establishing maps and claims in present day California as early as 1602 and launching military expeditions as far north as Nebraska, where in 1720 a French and Pawnee allied force finally halted Spain's territorial advancement into New France. Spanish colonial expeditions after the voyages of Columbus at first utilized a flag depicting a red Cross of St. Andrew on a field of white, although there were many variations in color, shape and adornments to this flag. Unlike the Scottish St. Andrew's Cross Flag, the Spanish versions of the flag usually depicted rough or knotted cross bars. **The Spanish Flag of Burgundy** was carried by expeditions throughout what is now the Western United States, and many such flags were presented to Native American tribes along the way, a practice later adopted from the Spanish by the English and Americans.

 5 Spanish explorer Bruno de Heceta reached the present day Washington coast in 1775 aboard the Spanish ship *Santiago*. The Spaniards sent ships back in 1790 and 1791. To avoid confusion with the traditional Flag of England, in the 1790's The Spanish Flag of Burgundy was changed to **The Spanish Maritime Ensign** in its North American colonies.

 6 When the earliest French explorer Giovanni da Verrazano sailed along the upper North American coast from present-day North Carolina to New York in March, 1524, he carried **The French Fleurs-de-lis Flag with a Field of Blue**. This was the original flag of New France on the North American Continent.

7 After 1589, and until the French Revolution (1789), the French Bourbon Dynasty's **French Fleurs-de-lis Flag with a Field of White** hosted the fleurs-de-lis ("lily flowers"), either three in number or many superimposed over a field of white. This version of The French Fleurs-de-lis Flag was the French Army Flag of New France west of the Appalachian Mountains chain during the North American French and Indian War (1754-1763).

 8 When the English explorer John Cabot discovered the North American Continent in 1497, his vessel carried **The English Cross of St. George Flag**. This flag brought the first English colonists to Jamestown in 1607 and to Plymouth in 1620.

 9 The English Cross of St. George Flag flew over the first English colonies in what was to become the United States until 1634 when the puritans refused to further display the flag on religious grounds that the "cross" was a sign of idolatry. Thereafter, individual colonies in New England fashioned their own **New England Pine Tree Flag**. The field of red on Pine Tree Flags was adopted from the British Maritime Ensign after 1707.

 10 In 1707, England (which had already annexed Wales) became "Great Britain" with the merger of the Scottish and English Parliaments. The flag of the new country became **The Great Britain Union Flag**, combining the English Cross of St. George on a field of white with the Scottish Cross of St. Andrew on a field of blue. A third red Cross of St. Patrick, said to symbolize Ireland, would not be added to The Great Britain Union Flag until 1801.

Flags of the American Revolution

 11 Beginning in the Sixteenth Century, English maritime fleets were customarily divided into three units or squadrons: the van, the center and the rear. Each fleet squadron flew a specified colored ensign, originally with the Cross of St. George in the canton. Thus, the van squadron of a fleet flew a flag with the Cross of St. George in the canton on a field of white, the rear squadron of a fleet (commanded by a "Rear Admiral") flew a flag with an identical canton but on a field of blue, and the center squadron of the fleet flew a flag with an identical canton but on a field of red. The center squadron, displaying the red field ensign, was assigned the highest ranking admiral who commanded the entire fleet. In 1707, the new Great Britain Union Flag became the canton of the three maritime flags, and the entire British merchant marine and all of Britain's overseas colonies in North America were ordered to fly the *red* **British Maritime Ensign**. The white and blue field maritime ensigns, along with the red, were still used by the British Navy. Therefore, as of 1707 the North American British colonies began to fly the red British Maritime Ensign as an official flag in colonial offices, many town greens, and on every colonial merchant marine and militia vessel. As the American Revolutionary War opened there was no flag signifying the united colonial effort to gain independence. The official flag of a British overseas colony was the British Maritime Ensign, and this flag was flown in many towns and cities in the American Colonies. Moreover, the British Maritime Ensign was flown by most of the American Colonies' ships of war throughout the Revolutionary War, probably to avoid the accusation of piracy on the high seas if found to be operating without a flag recognized internationally as from a sovereign nation. For this reason the British *red* Maritime Ensign is considered **The First Flag of the United States**.

12 The Sons of Liberty, also The True Born Sons of Liberty, The Sons of Freedom, The Liberty Boys, and even The Daughters of Liberty, were groups of scattered secret organizations throughout the American Colonies from August, 1765 on that rose up in protest to the British Stamp Act passed in the same year. Their original motto was invariably "no taxation without representation" but over the years the groups moved closer and closer to a revolutionary and independent America position. The original **Sons of Liberty Flag** had nine alternating red and white *vertical* stripes, representing the nine colonies which publicly opposed the Stamp Act of 1765.

13 At the outset of the Revolutionary War, town flags often sufficed – sometimes with slight modifications – as rallying banners for the growing conflict with the British. Because of the colonial self-imposed embargo on British cloth, materials to make flags were expensive and consisted of either modifications to existing flags or colonial "home spun". The town **Flag of Taunton Massachusetts** is a case in point. To express the town's anti-British sentiments, the British Maritime Ensign was hauled down, and the words "Liberty and Union" added to it on October 21, 1774. It was flown from the town's "Liberty Pole" on the square until the British policy arose of cutting down such flag poles in a vain attempt to prevent protest flags from being flown.

14 On July 23, 1776, when news of the signing of the Declaration of Independence reached the town of Huntington, New York, the town people hauled down the British Maritime Ensign, removed the British Union canton from the upper hoist corner and sewed on the word "Liberty" to their new, revolutionary town flag. **The Huntington Flag** was later carried into the Battle of Long Island by the 1st Regiment of the Suffolk County Militia, during which battle it was captured by Hessian troops. It survived in a German museum until World War II when it was destroyed in an allied fire bomb attack.

 15 When Paul Revere rallied the Massachusetts Militiamen to stand and oppose the British in the wee hours of April 19, 1775, the men of the Town of Bedford had no flag to lead their contingent of militiamen to Concord Bridge except the town's old flag which had been used in the French and Indian War by the local militia years before. Militiaman Nathaniel Page grabbed the flag from the town hall and ran with it to Concord Bridge and the ensuing battle, christening **The Bedford Flag** as "The First Battle Flag of the United States". The Latin phrase on the flag "VINCE AUT MORIRE" means "Conquer or Die".

 16 A version of the New England Pine Tree Flag, called **The New England Battle Flag**, was carried at the Battle of Bunker Hill (actually fought on neighboring Breed's Hill), but the specific version of the flag remains in dispute. For many years, a 19th Century pictured version of the flag with a blue field was thought to be a printer's error due to a faded lithograph model he examined to re-produce the famous flag in a textbook, especially in light of the fact that Colonel John Trumbull's famous painting *"The Death of Warren"* (1786) depicting the Battle of Bunker Hill showed the colonists carrying the red field version – that is until historians made two observations. First, it was clear that Trumbull was no expert about flags. Even the British flag depicted in the painting was not a British Army flag at the time. The flag depicted on the British side of the painting is the British Maritime Ensign, not the flag of the British Army. More importantly, a letter surfaced from an eyewitness at the time which clearly described the Bunker Hill flag as having a *blue* field.

17 During the Siege of Boston in September 1775, the Americans launched two floating batteries on the Charles River to harry British positions inside the city. In October 1775, Commander-in-Chief Washington commissioned two schooners armed with cannon, the *Lynch* and the *Franklin*, to cruise Boston Bay. Both of the floating batteries and the two schooners flew **The Appeal to Heaven Flag** designed by Washington. By February 1776 a total of six armed vessels of the "United Colonies of North America" had been financed and commissioned by Washington, all flying the flag. The phrase "an appeal to heaven" did not have religious connotations but referred to John Locke's famous *Two Treatises of Government* in which Locke suggested *natural law*, or idiomatically "an appeal to heaven"(as to the proper course of action), is the only thing left to do when reason and negotiation have failed with one's enemies. On July 26, 1776, the Massachusetts Assembly made the Appeal to Heaven Flag the official flag of the colony's navy. The flag was popular, with some variations containing the words "We Appeal to Heaven", "Appeal to God", or simply "Appeal to Heaven".

18 All American Colonies used maritime ensigns and jacks which flew on their commercial seagoing vessels, many of which were armed for defense. George Washington's Military Secretary, Colonel Joseph Reed, proposed that all American Revolutionary War ships fly the older version of The Massachusetts Navy Flag, now called **The New England Ensign**. They didn't.

19 Combining the thirteen alternating red and white stripes symbolizing the American Colonies with the British Union canton, George Washington referred to this flag as **The Great Union Flag**, and it was his personal favorite of all of the flags of the American Revolution. Although it was never officially adopted by the Continental Congress, on

January 1, 1776, this flag was first formally raised on Prospect Hill in Somerville, Massachusetts at the formal commissioning of the Continental Army which had come into existence on June 14, 1775. Thus, it was the land military's official national colors which General Washington was fully authorized to establish. Today, this flag is usually referred to as the "Grand Union Flag," and it was the first flag of the new nation to be officially saluted by a foreign government, on November 16, 1776.

 20 The militia called the Green Mountain Boys was from the area now comprising the State of Vermont, and it used this well-known unit flag which is still the flag of the Vermont State Guard. The Green Mountain Boys under **The Green Mountain Boys Flag** were successful in capturing Fort Ticonderoga and Fort Crown Point from the British. On August 17, 1776, John Stark led the militia under this flag to defeat British General Johnny Burgoyne in the Battle of Bennington.

 21 Colonel William Moultrie of South Carolina was commissioned in 1775 to head the Second South Carolina Regiment, and in 1776 his colonial militia led a gallant and successful defense of Charleston, South Carolina, turning back the British forces of Sir Henry Clinton and Sir Peter Parker, and earning Moultrie a promotion to Brigadier General in the Continental Army. His South Carolina militia wore helmets with half moons inscribed with the word "Liberty" during the defense of Charleston, which crescents may have been from the coats of arms of founding fathers of the colony who were "second sons" of the gentry (*i.e.,* those not inheriting land). The South Carolina Militia fashioned a flag with a crescent moon and the word "Liberty" to hoist over their batteries as they fired on the British attacking Charleston. Historians are divided over whether the historic **Moultrie Flag**

had the word "Liberty" exterior to the crescent moon or within it as the helmet emblem did.

 **22 The Guilford Courthouse Flag** was carried by the North Carolina Militia at the famous and important Battle of Guilford Courthouse, North Carolina, on March 15, 1781. In the battle a numerically superior force of Continental Army units and militiamen lead by America's brilliant tactician General Nathaneal Greene held in wooded fixed positions and along a fence line as a large contingent of British General Cornwallis' forces advanced. When the British troops had advanced to within 50 yards of the Americans and theoretical musket range British Lt. Colonel James Webster ordered his men to run at the American lines, an order which not only cost Webster his own life, but resulted in 25% British casualties within two or three minutes. As the British retreated in confusion General Greene abruptly withdrew the American forces according to the Continental Army battle plan – leading a humiliated General Cornwallis to claim a technical victory. Following announcement of the huge British casualties, Whig politician Charles Fox rose in British Parliament in London to say, "[O]ne more such 'victory' as this and the British Army will be finished!"

 23 The Join or Die Flag was not originally thematically presented *via* a flag, but appeared as a political cartoon created by Benjamin Franklin, and was first published in the *Pennsylvania Gazette* on May 9, 1754. Franklin was part owner of the newspaper. This cartoon is the earliest known depiction of the snake political theme in America, and in 1754 it was used to inspire unity in the colonies in the French and Indian War (1754-1763) to combat common foes. In 1765 the segmented snake theme took on a new meaning. This time the British Government was the common enemy as drawings of it were circulated in protest of the British Stamp Act and to popularize the Stamp Act Congress of October 19, 1765, a precursor to the First Continental Congress.

 **24** As Commodore Esek Hopkins readied the first Continental Navy fleet to attack the British, at first he ordered American naval vessels to fly a "striped" jack on their bow in support of the revolutionary cause, the stripes symbolizing the 13 American colonies. This was **The Traditional Naval Jack** of the American Navy. However, as things turned out, it wasn't the first Naval Jack to fly in battle.

 25 To the symbolism of the rattlesnake flag lore, we must thank the first units of the American Marines for the words "Don't Tread on Me." In the fall of 1775 the Continental Congress authorized the formation of the first five companies of Marines to serve with the newly formed Continental Navy. The first Marine units from Philadelphia carried marching drums depicting a rattlesnake with the motto "Don't Tread On Me" printed on the drums. Before the first Continental Navy fleet set sail, Colonel Christopher Gadsden, a member of the Continental Congress from the Colony of South Carolina, presented Commodore Hopkins with a yellow flag depicting a coiled rattlesnake and the Marines' warning phrase on the field. The Commodore loved **The Gadsden Flag** and immediately adopted it as his personal colors.

 **26** Before the first Continental Navy fleet sailed, Commodore Hopkins ordered that the fleet's revolutionary naval jacks be modified, to sew rattlesnakes and warning phrases on them similar to his Gadsden Flag. By tradition (and a very strong naval tradition at that), the **First American Naval Jack** contained the rattlesnake and the warning phrase on it as the Continental Navy fleet attacked the British-held Bahamas, and as the American Marines made their first beach landing in the Battle of Nassau on March 3, 1776.

 27 Commodore Hopkins' initial brilliant victories against the British were followed by a series of disappointments (including a British blockade of most of his fleet), and on January 2, 1778, he was relieved of his command by Congress. Not only Commodore Hopkins, but also The First Naval Jack fell out of favor, with Continental Navy vessels flying a new version of the naval jack by late 1777. The new Naval Jack was a field of blue upon which were placed 13 stars signifying the American Colonies. New Stars were added as new States entered the Union. This was the **U.S. Naval Jack** until May 31, 2002, when the Secretary of the Navy ordered that Commodore Hopkins' First Naval Jack again be flown on all American naval vessels for the duration of the Global War on Terrorism. So, the First Naval Jack is again the official jack of the American Navy.

 28 At the time Colonel Christopher Gadsden presented The Gadsden Flag to Commodore Hopkins in 1775, he also presented a duplicate of it to the South Carolina Assembly, which made an official entry about the gift into the Assembly's records and ordered that a modification of it similar to Hopkins' jack fly as **The South Carolina Colonial Naval Jack** during the Revolutionary War.

29 Other American colonial units adopted the rattlesnake theme for their flags as well. One such flag, **The Culpeper Minutemen Flag**, was carried by a group "of about one hundred minutemen" from Culpeper, Virginia, in 1775. They became a part of Patrick Henry's First Virginia Regiment, and later the Virginia Line of the Continental Army.

 30 Ship chandlers (suppliers) in the Port of Philadelphia described a Grand Union Flag with various color stripes ordered for Commodore Hopkins' Continental Navy fleet during the winter of 1776-1777. Because of the different colored stripes, **The Hopkins Fleet Flags** were perhaps used in signaling of some kind.

 31 The first *U.S.S. Lexington* was the brigantine *Wild Duck* purchased by the Continental Congress and renamed *Lexington* in 1776 in honor of the famous battle which had brought the revolutionaries to the point of political exile and potential death at the hands of the British authorities. Outfitted with 16 guns, the *Lexington* had a distinguished and storybook career engaging the British in the Revolutionary War under three separate captains until, becalmed and out of powder near the English Channel, she was seriously damaged and captured by the British cutter *Alert* on September 19, 1777. **The Lexington Flag** combined the British Maritime Ensign's canton with 13 stripes (not drastically different than Washington's Grand Union Flag) and may have been flown as an ensign resembling the British flag "close enough" to avoid piracy claims.

32 The famous Serapis Flag was described by Benjamin Franklin in a letter to the King of Naples as the "Flag of the United States" in 1778. In 1779 Commodore John Paul Jones put to sail in the new colonial warship *The Bonhomme Richard* to harass British shipping off the coast of England and occasionally shell English ports. His new frigate was named in Franklin's honor and carried the flag described by Franklin. In the fierce and famous sea battle of the American vessels *Bonhomme Richard* and *Alliance* with the British frigate *Serapis* in the English Channel on September 23, 1779, as the *Bonhomme Richard* began to sink, the British commander noticed the American jack had disappeared from its mast, and shouted to Commodore Jones, "Sir, are you striking your colors?" (Meaning, "do you surrender?") Jones famously shouted back, "No, Sir, I have not yet begun to fight, and we are coming aboard your vessel." With support fire from the American frigate *Alliance,* Jones ordered his men to fight their way aboard the British vessel as their own sank, and after a hand-to-hand battle the Americans successfully commandeered the *Serapis*, hoisting **The Serapis Flag** from the main mast in place of the British Maritime Ensign.

 33 Following the famous battle with the British 44-gun frigate *Serapis* on September 23, 1779, and now oblivious to the dangers of piracy since the British listed him as such, John Paul Jones took over command of the American 36-gun support frigate *Alliance* in Texel Roads, Netherlands, as the British fleet with several Ships of the Line moved in to blockade his leaving the port. Under cover of several Dutch Ships of the Line, John Paul Jones hoisted **The Alliance Flag** from the main mast of his vessel and slipped out of the roads to again harass British shipping. The Alliance Flag is superficially similar to the final version of the American Flag used today. However, there were 13 stripes with white *exterior* stripes instead of red, and the stars were eight pointed instead of five. Captain John Paul Jones would never again fly the British Maritime Ensign in accommodation to the International Law of Nations. His fleet vessels now represented "United America."

34 A "privateer" referred to individuals or companies who equipped their own vessels with weapons and raided enemy merchant and naval shipping for a profit under *Letters of Marque & Reprisal* issued by a country at war, and in the case of America by the revolutionary Continental Congress. In the Revolutionary War, 55,000 Americans served as crews aboard 1,700 privateer vessels. In the course of the Revolutionary War, American privateers captured 2,283 British merchant and military ships, which they hauled into American held, French, Dutch and Spanish ports, claiming war "prize". The captured ships and cargoes would then be sold at auction with the proceeds divided between the privateers and the Continental Congress to re-invest in the war effort. Privateer vessels did not much care about the International Law of Nations and its flag requirements since they knew the British would hang them as pirates if they were captured in any event. American privateer ships brazenly hoisted stylized ensigns from their main masts consisting of stars and stripes in a variety of designs. While at port in Martinique in 1776, the American privateer brig *Reprisal* was witnessed flying **The Privateer Flag** of 13 yellow and black stripes, perhaps symbolic of the (black) pirate and (yellow) plague on board colors.

35 The Philadelphia Light Horse Flag represented a Light Horse unit formed by Philadelphians at their own expense who supplied their own horses and equipment. In June 1775 they escorted General Washington from Philadelphia to Cambridge, Massachusetts for the formation of the Continental Army on the 14th. The Philadelphia Light Horse fought in the battles of Brandywine, Germantown, Princeton and Trenton, and probably in others as well.

 36 From 1724 to the 1750's settlers from the colonies of New York and New Hampshire arrived in the area now known as the State of Vermont, leading to conflicting claims to the new settlements by the two colonies. In 1764 the British Crown adjudicated the dispute in favor of New York, which decision then led to a long standing dispute between New York and the settlers themselves who wanted independent status as a colony. Despite its heroic service in the Revolutionary War, the Continental Congress refused to recognize the new jurisdiction on the basis of New York's objection. On January 15, 1777, representatives from the area declared themselves independent from both New York and the colonies united by the Continental Congress, as the "Republic of New Connecticut." The independent republic's name was changed to the "Republic of Vermont" six months later, from the French *les Verts Monts*, or "the Green Mountains". The official **Flag of the Republic of Vermont** was that of its Green Mountain Boys Militia. The Republic of Vermont would operate as an independent nation until 1791 when it joined the Union as one of the United States

Flags of the New American Nation

 37 By resolution dated June 14, 1777 (traditionally "Flag Day" in the United States), the Marine Committee of the Second Continental Congress declared simply: *"Resolved, that the flag of the United States be thirteen stripes, alternate red and white; that the union [canton] be thirteen stars, white in a blue field representing a new constellation."* The flag with a circle of thirteen stars on a blue canton and thirteen stripes appeared soon thereafter and was even placed anachronistically in paintings depicting earlier events. Until the Flag Act of 1794 this flag was (correctly so) referred to as **The Naval Ensign of the United States**. Congress never formally adopted an official flag for the Army of the United States. By default and custom, the Naval Ensign became **The First National Flag of the United States** by 1781.

 **38** After being pursued and outflanked near Cowpens, South Carolina, by a British force under the command of Lt. Colonel "Benny" Tarleton, Continental Brigadier General Daniel Morgan – an experienced military tactician from the time of the French and Indian War – decided to let his mixed force of nearly 2,000 experienced continentals and local militiamen be "trapped" by the enemy. As the British charged the American lines the front two rows of militia men fired two rounds and seemed to flee toward their left by the hundreds. Encouraged, the British charged forward only to discover Morgan's battle hardened Continental regulars in a third line charging straight at them, with fixed bayonets, on the heels of the militiamen. With the British now in the midst of the Americans, the militiamen themselves turned, en masse, with fixed bayonets, as American Lt. Colonel William Washington (General George Washington's cousin) charged out from the rear of the continentals with 80

cavalry to cut off the British retreat on the right. Shocked by the ferocity of the bayonet attacks, over 700 of the British who were not killed threw down their weapons and surrendered. **The Cowpens Flag** carried by the Continental Army was a variation of the Betsy Ross design authorized by the Maritime Committee of the Second Continental Congress on June 14, 1777. In flag history The Cowpens Flag is an important milestone, showing that in the three years following the first unveiling of the Betsy Ross Stars and Stripes, the flag had become so popular as to have replaced the Great Union Flag in the Continental Army.

 39 By the Flag Act of 1794, and to reflect the entry of Vermont (1791) and Kentucky (1792) into the Union, the number of stripes of the First National Flag of the United States (June 14, 1777) was increased from 13 to 15, and the field of stars was increased as well in the canton. This famous fifteen stripes, fifteen stars flag, popularly known as **The Star Spangled Banner**, was the United States flag during the War of 1812. During the British shelling of Fort McHenry in Baltimore Harbor for 25 continuous hours commencing September 12, 1814, an oversized Star Spangle Banner, named "the Great Garrison Flag", flew over the ramparts of the fort. Upon seeing the flag during the battle from his position on a truce ship in the harbor, Francis Scott Key wrote a poem he entitled "Defense of Ft. McHenry" which was subsequently re-titled "The Star Spangled Banner" and put to music to the tune of "Anacreon in Heav'n". The song eventually became the National Anthem of the United States.

40 In the War of 1812, "Don't give up the ship" were the dying words of American Captain James Lawrence during the naval battle between the *USS Chesapeake* and *HMS Shannon* on June 1, 1813, which battle was ironically lost resulting in the capture of the *Chesapeake*. Nevertheless, American Commodore Oliver

Hazard Perry placed the saying on a field of blue, and it became the Commodore's personal battle Flag. The *USS Niagara* flew the **Commodore Perry Battle Flag** at the Battle of Lake Erie (September 10, 1813) in which an American squadron of nine vessels captured an entire British squadron of warships, reportedly the only time in history an entire squadron of the British Navy has been captured intact.

41 The Free Trade and Sailors Rights Flag of the War of 1812 was somewhat of an unlucky banner on American warships, being flown by both the *USS Chesapeake* when it was captured on June 1, 1813, and the *USS Essex* when it was captured on March 28, 1814.

42 The Lewis & Clark Expedition to explore the Missouri River headwaters and the Louisiana Purchase (1803), and which began May 14, 1804, carried many flags with it intended to be presentation gifts to the Native Americans it would encounter. The expedition was a United States Army project, and both Lewis and Clark were army officers. **The Lewis and Clark Expedition Flag** they carried was the flag of the American Army at the time. This flag had fifteen stripes of the Star Spangled Banner and seventeen stars representing the seventeen states of the Union at that time. It was quite elongated. Flag variations such as this were not unusual for this time period. Congress would not definitively direct the number of stars and stripes on a flag until 1818. The dimensions and colors of the American flag would not be standardized until after World War II, and then for flags used only by the Federal Government.

43 John Charles Frémont (January 21, 1813 – July 13, 1890), known to the popular press in his own time as "The Pathfinder", lead important expeditions to the American West of the Oregon Trail (1842), the Oregon Territory (1844), and the Arkansas River Headwaters (1845). Fremont was a commissioned officer in the United States Army Engineering Corps with map-making skills. On his journeys of exploration, Fremont carried a specially designed 26 star **Fremont Expedition Flag** that his wife Bessie had hand sewn. The canton of this flag was a version of the eagle-motif United States Army Flag in the 1840's, with the customary olive branch clutched in the claws of the eagle being replaced with a calumet which Fremont hoped would be interpreted as a peace sign by the Native American hostiles he met.

 44 Shortly before his murder in 1844, Joseph Smith, Jr., gave the Church of Latter Day Saints explicit instructions as to the making of an organizational flag, which instructions were carried out after his death. Mormon symbolism embodied in the flag is extensive and may be subject to on-going interpretation. However, it is fairly clear that the *twelve* alternating stripes and the circle of *twelve* stars in the canton refer at least to the "Twelve Tribes of Israel". The center 13th canton star does not complete a political reference to the thirteen original American Colonies, but is said to allude to Jesus Christ as the center and head of the Twelve Tribes. Blue and white are colors of deep significance to the Church of Latter Day Saints. Brigham Young, successor to Smith, reported shortly after Smith's death that he had received a vision in which he had seen **The Mormon Pioneer Flag** flying over a specific mountain at the precise place where the Mormon community ought go and would prosper if they did. Following John Fremont's published expedition account of the Utah Territory, when the Mormon pioneers arrived at the vista of the Great Salt Lake, Young in fact exclaimed "this is the place", perhaps in reference to the guiding vision he had seen. On July 29, 1847, the pioneer flag was raised over aptly named "Ensign Peak" at today's Salt Lake City.

 45 On July 27, 1810, English and American settlers along the Gulf Coast regions of West Florida, Alabama, Mississippi and Louisiana to the Mississippi River at Baton Rouge declared themselves the independent Republic of West Florida, and hoisted **The Bonnie Blue Flag** bearing a single star, which was to play a major role in the histories of Texas and South Carolina. Exactly 90 days after the Republic of West Florida declared itself an independent republic, the United States annexed it, claiming it had been a part of the Louisiana Purchase from France in 1803. However, it most certainly had not been a part of the purchase. New France included only those lands which were drained naturally by the Mississippi River and its tributaries, and the rivers of the Republic of West Florida ran from North to South into the Gulf of Mexico, not the Mississippi River. Disagreements between the United States and Spain continued until 1819 and the Adams-Onis Treaty when the matter was settled diplomatically – but not on the basis of geography – in favor of the United States.

 **46** From the Flag Act of 1794 until April 4, 1818 the flag was not changed at all despite the entry of five new states to the Union on the historical assumption that adding new stripes and new stars with each new state's admission would create visual clutter. On April 4, 1818, Congress addressed the United States Flag for the first time in a quarter century, and at the suggestion of a naval captain, Samuel Reid, directed that the number of stars in the flag reflect the number of states in the Union, but the stripes would be permanently reduced from fifteen to thirteen in honor of the original 13 colonies of the United States. Thus, in 1818,

30

The 20 Star Flag set the numerical stripes and stars pattern for all future Flags of the United States.

47 As was the case with the original flag resolution of the Second Continental Congress in 1777, neither the 1818 Law nor any law since has mandated a specific *arrangement* of the stars of the American flag, leaving open various designs that were popular in the 19th Century as alternates to a rectangular pattern. The 20 Star Flag itself was made in a popular pattern at the time, **The Great Star Flag**.

48 The Bennington Flag, despite its name and despite the myth which grew up about it in the 19th Century, was not carried by the grandfather of President Millard Fillmore at the Battle of Bennington (fought in New York) on August 16, 1777. Analysis of the original flag's material revealed that it was a 19th Century production, probably created for either the American 1826 Fifty Year or 1876 Centennial Celebrations. It is nevertheless a striking, patriotic and beautiful American Flag still popular over a century after its design.

49 Early American settlers to California initially attempted to revolt from Mexico in 1836, led by fur trader and mountain man Isaac Graham (1800-1863). The revolt raised **The Red Star Flag** as its standard. Graham declared California an independent republic for a few hours before he and his followers (including a few British Nationals) were arrested and thrown into a Mexican prison, causing an International incident.

50 John Fremont's Third Expedition to the West was supposed to end at the headwaters of the Arkansas River, but when he reached them in present day Colorado, without orders he continued with his band of 55 men on to Central California in early 1846 and began inciting the Americans there to revolt against Mexico. At first, Fremont's attempts to incite a second revolution in California seemed as futile as the first revolution had been. The Mexican Army chased him into the Oregon Territory where his group stayed until Californians did rise up against the Mexicans on June 14, 1846, declaring California an independent republic and hoisting **The Bear Flag of The Second California Republic**. What the new nation of the California Republic didn't know was that the United States had already declared War on Mexico on May 13, 1846, but news didn't reach California until 26 days after the revolution when a frigate and two sloops from the United States Navy arrived in Montery Bay, took control of California, and cut down the The Bear Flag from its pole, thus ending California's short lived independence.

Flags of the Texas Independence Struggles

 51 The Adams-Onis Treaty of 1819 established the Sabine River (the present eastern border of the State of Texas) as the boundary line between the United States and Spanish possessions to the west. The treaty was extremely unpopular among some American pioneers who either had settled in the Eastern Texas area or were planning to, among whom was Dr. James Long, a former United States Army veteran from the War of 1812. In 1819, Long led a group of settlers in a successful attack on the Spanish East Texas town of Nacogdoches where he proclaimed the independent "Republic of Texas" and was immediately elected as the new republic's first president. Within a month Long and his men were chased back into the United States by a Spanish Army detachment. Long's **First Republic of Texas Flag** is the ancestor of the Texas "Lone Star" which is prominent on so many of its historical flags.

 52 Just as the War for Mexican Independence was ending in favor of an independent United Mexican States, Long returned to East Texas in 1821 with a militia of 300 armed men bearing a new, **(Second) First Republic of Texas Flag** sewn by his wife Jane. Long and his militia succeeded in seizing the fortress at present day Goliad in Southeast Texas before being captured and thrown into a Mexican prison, where Long was summarily shot six months later.

 53 Following the (successful) Mexican War of Independence from Spain (1810-1821) debate ensued among the revolutionaries as to whether a strong centralized government along European lines or a confederation of individually sovereign states was the superior mechanism of governance. At first, the pro-confederation forces won out, and the 19 states and 3 territories of the United Mexican States became each "free, sovereign and independent" governments under the first Constitution of Mexico (1824). The "Federalists" or "Conservative Texans", among who was land magnate Stephen F. Austin, supported the Constitution of 1824, and raised **The 1824 Flag** in support of continued union with Mexico.

 **54** Under the Constitution of 1824 most American-Texans who had settled in the Mexican State of Coahuila y Tejas were delighted because they basically had home rule of their own affairs. The Mexican State of Coahuila y Tejas even had its own militia, largely manned by American-Texan settlers. The two stars of **The Coahuila y Tejas Militia Flag** stood for the joint United Mexican State of Coahuila and Tejas.

55 On December 21, 1826, American settlers in the vicinity of Nacogdoches, Mexican East Texas, again raised a flag of revolution and declared their independence from the United Mexican States. They formed a new country named the "Republic of Fredonia" under the leadership of local land magnate Haden Edwards. The revolutionaries reportedly each signed the new **Flag of Fredonia** as a sign of their allegiance to the new republic. At this time most American-Texans were loyal citizens of the United Mexican States and backers of the Constitution of 1824. A revolt in Nacogdoches was considered a revolt against the sovereign state of Coahuila y Tejas, which the American-Texans were firmly in control of. 100 Mexican Army troops and 250 militiamen from Stephen Austin's American-Texan settlements entered the Republic of Fredonia, and by January 31, 1827 the Republic of Fredonia was no more. Edwards fled to the United States.

56 The American-Texans' loyalty to Mexico was tested when on September 15, 1829, Mexico's President Guerrero issued an Emancipation Proclamation outlawing slavery throughout Mexico and freeing all slaves held in captivity. By that time, 20% of the population of Coahuila y Tejas was slaves working on plantations set up on the American Deep South model. The slave holding American-Texans flatly refused to follow the new law, and many raised **The Liberals Independence Flag** for independence from Mexico, perhaps not entirely but in large measure over the issue of slavery.

57 In 1831 the Mexican Army had lent a small cannon to the Texas town militia of Gonzales for protection against Comanche raids, and as talk of Texas resistance to Mexico City policies increased in mid-1835, the Mexican Army, perhaps prudently, sent a detachment of 100 cavalry to Gonzales to get the cannon back. When the cavalry commander asked for the cannon, the townsmen, now aided with more armed Texans from the countryside, voted to barricade the town for an attack and pointed the cannon at the Mexicans. Behind the barricades, **The Come and Take It Flag** was hoisted up. The slogan itself was a Texan version of the Spartan's response to the Persian King Xerxes at the Battle of Thermopylae in 480 B.C.E. when he sent the Spartans a note telling them to lay down their weapons. The Spartans famously replied "Μολών λαβέ", or in English "come and get them." The Mexican cavalry finally had no option other than to charge the Gonzales barricades, and after two or three futile attempts they broke off the attack and left.

58 Three weeks after the canon incident in Gonzales, Texas, a coup in Mexico City dissolved the Federal Republic and abolished the Constitution of 1824. Five of the United Mexican

States immediately seceded from Mexico and established independent Republics, and Coahuila seceded from Tejas – leaving the Texans by themselves. The Texans themselves were nonetheless still split into two parties: those that favored re-instatement of the Constitution of 1824 and re-unification with Mexico, and the pro-slavery group that favored total Texas independence. This latter group was comprised of younger and much more aggressive individuals who quickly fashioned a new flag to represent their (renewed) calls for Texas independence, **The Dodson Flag**. On March 2, 1836, the young Liberals won out and Texas formally declared its independence from Mexico, hoisting The Dodson Flag from the building where the secessionists were meeting. The colors of the flag were meant to hearken back to the French Revolution of 1789.

 59 The siege and Battle of the Alamo was fought between February 23 and March 6, 1836, resulting in the deaths of all of the mission's defenders except two, a courier who had been dispatched for reinforcements before the final battle and either a slave or former slave of the Alamo's commander William Travis. However, the Texans' defeat in the Battle of the Alamo was just a temporary setback for the pro-slavery Texas faction favoring revolution and an independent country. The Alamo became a rallying cry for revolution, and any thoughts of reconciliation with a united Mexico were finally dismissed. After news of the defeat at the Battle of the Alamo reached the revolutionaries, they hastily wrote out and passed a constitution for the new independent Texas Republic they envisioned, and one in which a slave economy played a prominent role. As a triumph of independence, the revolutionaries formally adopted a new flag for their new country, **The Burnet Flag**, which was simply the Bonnie Blue Flag of the pro-slavery Liberals changed to bear a single *gold* star.

 **60** During the Texas War of Independence, revolutionary fever among many Texans hearkened back to the by-gone days of James Long and the First Republic of Texas, and some militia units and Texas communities began to fly an unofficial variation of that flag, dubbed **The Lone Star and Stripes Flag**.

 61 On January 25, 1839, the Republic of Texas officially adopted a new flag which combined the Bonnie Blue and Dodson Flags of the Liberals, and even harkened back to the "Lone Star" first flag of the First Republic of Texas. The Republic of Texas existed from March 2, 1836 to December 29, 1845, and for over nine years Texas was an independent country. The United States recognized it as a foreign power, as did France, Belgium and the Netherlands. Mexico, as can be expected, did not recognize Texas as a separate country, and it continued to fight periodic military engagements with Texas. **The Flag of the Republic of Texas** became the Flag of the State of Texas when negotiations culminated on December 29, 1845 for annexation of Texas by the United States of America. The new State of Texas became the 28th Star on the American Flag.

Flags of the American Civil War

 62 When South Carolina became the first State of the Union to secede on December 20, 1860, it declared itself to be the independent Republic of South Carolina, popularly known in the Southern United States as the "Palmetto Republic". The South Carolina legislature took the issue of what its new flag should be quite seriously and debated the issue extensively. The legislature finally settled on a version of the Moultrie Flag from the Revolutionary War (a crescent in a field of blue) further embellished with a palmetto tree in honor of the fact that Colonel Moultrie had used palmetto logs in the fort he constructed to defend Charleston. **The Republic of South Carolina Flag** served the republic until February 8 of the following year when South Carolina joined the Confederate States of America.

 63 On January 9, 1861, Mississippi became the second State of the Union to secede, and from then until February 8, 1861, it operated as the Republic of Mississippi. **The Flag of the Republic of Mississippi** included as its canton the "Bonnie Blue Flag" with a single star reminiscent of the West Florida Republic (1810), the Texas Republic (1836-1839) and the recent South Carolina Secession (1860) flags.

 64 On January 10, 1861, Florida became the third State of the Union to secede, and from then until February 8, 1861, it operated as the Republic of Florida. **The Republic of Florida Flag** it adopted during this brief period was a version of an unofficial flag of the Republic of Texas, and the maritime ensign Texas had used during its Independent Republic Period.

65 Alabama voted to secede from the Union on January 11, 1861, and the Secession Convention immediately commissioned a flag for the independent Alabama Republic. A committee of women from Montgomery designed and constructed a complicated two-sided flag for the new republic. The obverse side of the flag depicted "Lady Liberty" holding the familiar Bonnie Blue Flag of the West Florida Republic over which "Alabama" was written, and contained the motto "Independent Now and Forever." The reverse side of the flag depicted a cotton plant and coiled snake with the motto "Noli Me Tangere" in Latin, or "touch me not." **The Republic of Alabama Flag** was badly damaged after a single display (during a thunder storm) and was never duplicated or flown again. The Alabama Republic lasted only until February 18, 1861 and Alabama's entry into the Confederacy.

 66 On January 26, 1861, Louisiana became the sixth State of the Union to secede, and for two weeks until February 8, 1861, when it joined the Confederacy it operated as the Republic of Louisiana. **The Republic of Louisiana Flag** was essentially Dr. James Long's 1821 Republic of Texas Flag with a gold colored star (instead of white) and an alternating blue stripe added. Long had been a Natchez, Mississippi plantation owner and had fought in the Battle of New Orleans (1815). He probably had many Louisiana contacts and was seen as a local martyred hero for independence.

 67 Following North Carolina's secession from the Union on May 20, 1861, its legislature adopted **The North Carolina Secession Flag** on June 22. The flag generally followed the Republic of Texas model with tri-colors and the lone star of secession. Two dates appeared in the canton. The May 20, 1775 date called to mind the so-called

Mecklenburg Declaration of Independence which North Carolinians believed predated the Declaration of Independence in the Revolutionary War. The second date recorded the Act of Secession, linking the Revolutionary War's goal of independence with the State's 1861 withdrawal from the Union.

 68 The State of Tennessee seceded from the Union on June 8, 1861, and although a flag was proposed for the new Confederate State, it was never officially adopted. **The Proposed Secession Flag of Tennessee** was a variation of the First Official Flag of the Confederacy (the "Stars and Bars") with the State Seal of Tennessee in the canton. Fringe trimmed its non-hoist edges.

 69 Many States of the Union did not have official flags of their own jurisdictions before the 20th Century, but revolutions, secession, and periods of independence brought with them the conviction that a flag apart from that of the United States was necessary to distinguish their territories from the rest of the (united) country. Although Virginia officially seceded from the Union on April 17, 1861, and joined the Confederate States of America a week later, as secession approached it had already adopted an official flag on January 13 of the same year. The flag features the seal of Virginia on a field of blue with the motto "Sic semper tyrannis" at the bottom, which was the phrase attributed to Brutus at the occasion of the assassination of Julius Caesar: "Thus always to tyrants." It is unclear as to what tyrant the motto was referring, as even the most likely suspect in the person of President Lincoln had not even taken office at the time the flag was adopted. The flag remains **The Commonwealth Flag of Virginia**, and is usually decorated with white fringe along the fly edge.

 **70** There were thirty-three stars and thirteen stripes on the United States flag at the commencement of the Civil War, and several star patterns were popular for American Flags. During the attack upon Ft. Sumter (April 12–13, 1861) near Charleston, South Carolina, which attack began the Civil War, **The Diamond Pattern 33 Star Flag** was flown at the Federal institution.

 **71** The "single star" **Bonnie Blue Flag** was the first unofficial flag of the Confederacy. It was **The Secessionist Flag of South Carolina** flown from the Confederate batteries during the attack upon Ft. Sumter (April 12–13, 1861). The Bonnie Blue Flag was a rallying banner in the first months of the rebellion. The Bonnie Blue Flag was, of course, the same flag as that of the short-lived Republic of West Florida (July 27 – October 27, 1810) which, for some inexplicable reason captured the imaginations of revolutionaries and secessionists from Texas to the Eastern Seaboard of the United States for over half a century in the early 1800's.

 72 Before Abraham Lincoln had even taken office, following the election of 1860 seven deep-south states seceded from the Union. South Carolina became the first state to secede (on December 20, 1860), followed by Mississippi, Florida, Alabama, Georgia, Louisiana and Texas. On February 4, 1861, these seven states formed the Confederate States of America, and on March 4, 1861 in Montgomery, Alabama the new nation in rebellion adopted its first flag, popularly known as the "Stars and Bars", **The First Official Flag of the Confederacy.**

73 & 74 Early variations of the Stars and Bars included seven stars for the first seven states in rebellion – or conversely fifteen stars on the assumption that all fifteen slave states would eventually join the Confederacy (two slave States, Delaware and Maryland, did not). After South Carolina's attack on the Federal installation at Ft. Sumter on April 12, 1861, four more states (Virginia, Arkansas, North Carolina and Tennessee) joined the Confederacy, and the stars on **The Nine & Eleven Star Confederate Stars and Bars Flag** jumped in two stages to eleven.

 75 After John Fremont's career as an explorer ended, he rose to prominence as an outspoken anti-slavery advocate and became the first member of the Republican Party to run for President in the election of 1856, on an explicit anti-slavery platform and using the slogan "Freedom, Free Men, and Frémont". He placed second to James Buchanan. When the Civil War began Fremont was recalled to service as a Major General and given jurisdiction over the Department of the West from May until November of 1861 with headquarters in the State of Missouri. His appointment was highly inflammatory. Within a month of Fremont's appointment, the State of Missouri seceded from the Union, becoming the 12th star on **The Thirteen Star Confederate Stars and Bars Flag**. Kentucky soon thereafter became the 13th Confederate star. After bizarrely punitive measures were ordered for the civilian population of Missouri by Fremont, he was replaced.

 **76** As soon as South Carolina seceded from the Union and withdrew its two senators from Congress, the voting block to prohibit Kansas from entering the Union as a non-slave State was broken. Kansas became the thirty-fourth state of the Union on January 29, 1861,

and **The 34 Star Flag** was authorized to be flown. The Federal government did not recognize the legality of the southern states' secessions, of course, and never reduced the star count on the Federal flag or its naval jacks used during the War.

 **77** On October 24, 1861, 41 counties in Northwest Virginia voted to form a new state separate from Virginia which by then had seceded from the Union. Voter turnout represented approximately 1/3 of eligible voters, Union troops prohibited pro-Virginia sympathizers from voting, and occupying federals actually voted in large numbers themselves at many polling places. The provisional name of the new state "Kanawha" was subsequently changed to "West Virginia". West Virginia's secession from Virginia and new statehood was recognized by Presidential Proclamation on April 20, 1863, without action by Congress, and the following 4th of July (1863) West Virginia became the 35th star on **The 35 Star Flag**.

 78 Although it was the first official governmental flag of the Confederacy, there were practical problems with the Stars and Bars Flag from the very beginning. At the First Battle of Manassas (also known as the First Battle of Bull Run) on July 21, 1861, the similarity between the flag of the United States and the Stars and Bars caused confusion and military problems. At a distance it was difficult for commanders to distinguish between the two flags, and units engaging each other became a visual jumble for field commanders' spotters. After the battle, Confederate General P. G. T. Beauregard declared that he was "resolved then to have [the flag] changed if possible, or to adopt for my command a battle flag, which would be entirely different from any State or Federal flag." His suggestion to change the Confederate National Flag was rejected, but the rejection made General Beauregard's intention to adopt distinct battle flags for the Confederacy prophetic. On

November 28, 1861, Confederate soldiers in the Army of Northern Virginia received the new battle flag in ceremonies at Centerville and Manassas, Virginia, and the Army carried the flag throughout the Civil War. After Confederate General Joseph Johnston took command of the Army of Tennessee, he adopted **The Confederate Battle Flag** as his army's colors too from 1864 until the end of the war in 1865.

 79 Despite the Confederate Congress' initial rejection of P.T. Beauregard's design request for a Confederate National Flag, by 1863 the General's Battle Flag used by his own army was so popular in the South that the official Confederate Flag design was changed on May 26, 1863 to incorporate the Battle Flag as a canton on a field of white, said to signify the "purity of the cause." **The Second Official Flag of the Confederacy** was popularly referred to as the "Stainless Banner".

 80 However, the Stainless Banner could also be mistaken on the battlefield or at sea as a flag of truce or surrender, and the South's generals and vessel captains objected vociferously. On March 4, 1865, the design was changed again. **The Third Official Flag of the Confederacy**, also called the "Blood Stained Banner", added a red stripe at the fly end of the flag. 35 days later the American Civil War ended.

 81 The Official Naval Jack of the Confederacy was an arrangement along the lines of the United States Naval Jack of the 19th Century, and had a varying number of stars on the field of blue, from seven to fifteen depending on the time the flag was made and the hopes and aspirations of the flag maker. Some Confederate naval vessels may have used the Confederate Battle Flag as a naval jack.

American National Flags of
the Late 19th & 20th Centuries

 **82 The 33 Star Flag** which flew from 1859 to 1861 came in at least four interesting versions, one of which was a star pattern in the canton – reminiscent but fuller than the Great Star Flag of 1818.

 **83** When President Lincoln was assassinated on April 14, 1865, Nevada had been admitted to the Union as the 36th State on the previous October 3rd, but the legal effective date for flying the 36 Star Flag would not happen until July 4, 1865. For the President's funeral an elegant 36 Star Flag was made with the arrangement of a star in the canton, and the flag was trimmed in black. **The Lincoln Funeral Flag**, the only one of its kind, was preserved and used for the funerals of every assassinated president since Lincoln, last flown during President John Kennedy's funeral.

 **84** Another interesting optional circle pattern of flag stars, hearkening back to the original authorized flag of the United States, re-emerged in the late 19th Century with the admission of Nevada and the creation of **The 36 Star Flag**, flown from July 4, 1865 to July 3, 1867.

 **85** In the early 19th Century, the United States Army adopted a new military flag consisting of a field of blue with an Eagle which was used until 1841 when this design was adopted as the basis for regimental guidons with personalized unit markings. Guidons were important field markings as battle flags in the 19th Century, and before. **The Standard United States Cavalry**

Guidon by 1876 was a stylized American Flag with "swallow tails". Several guidons of this design were carried by Lt. Colonel George Armstrong Custer's 7th Calvary Regiment at the Battle of Little Bighorn on June 25, 1876.

86 Colonel Custer's regiment also carried his personal swallow tailed red and blue guidon with crossed sabers. **Custer's Personal Guidon** was used to mark the Colonel's position, and it had been sewn together by his wife.

87 When Nebraska entered the Union, a double circle pattern of stars was possible on **The 37 Star Flag**, flown from July 4, 1867 to July 3, 1877.

88 When Colorado was admitted to the Union, an even more elaborate starburst pattern was developed for an optional **38 Star Flag** as opposed to the standard rectangle of stars, flown from July 4, 1877 to July 3, 1890.

89 When five States were all added to the Union in one year (Idaho, Washington, Montana, North Dakota and South Dakota) flag makers in the United States were caught by surprise as **The 43 Star Flag** had not been anticipated, because it was thought the Dakota Territory would enter the Union as a single State. Stockpiles of American flags had to be re-sewn to add an extra star before they could be sold.

90 By the time of the Spanish American War, the flag carried by Theodore Roosevelt in the charge up San Juan Hill was the **45 Star Flag**.

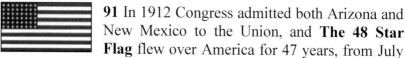 **91** In 1912 Congress admitted both Arizona and New Mexico to the Union, and **The 48 Star Flag** flew over America for 47 years, from July 4, 1912 to July 3, 1959 in the second longest period of one continuous flag configuration in America's history.

 **92** From July 4, 1959 to July 3, 1960, the American flag only had a new configuration for one year (49 stars with the admission of Alaska to the Union), but there have been seven such one-year periods in the county's history. From July 4, 1960 to the present day **The 50 Star Flag** has flown for the longest continual period in the nation's history.

American Military Branch Flags

93 The United States Army Flag has evolved over the years from its beginnings with General George Washington on January 1, 1776, through various stages of American Eagle motifs to its present appearance.

94 The United States Marine Corps began its proud history on November 10, 1775 with the commissioning of the first battalions of Continental Marines for the first Continental Navy. Throughout its history, the United States Marine Corps has created and utilized strong symbols pertaining to its mission, from its very first display of the coiled serpent and "Don't Tread On Me" imagery on its Corps drums in 1775. The current **United States Marine Corps Flag** carries on that tradition with its bold colors and graphic imagery.

95 On October 13, 1775, at the insistence of General George Washington who financed the very first war vessels of the United States himself, the United States Navy came into being just four months after the Continental Army was officially commisioned. **The United States Navy Flag** is one of many ensigns, jacks and flags the Navy has displayed over the two centuries of its service to the United States.

96 The United States Air Force Flag honors the relative newcomer to the military branches of the United States. The United States Air Force was officially created on September 18, 1947. Nevertheless, the Air Force traces its functional history to the Aeronautical Division of the United States Signal Corps in 1907.

97 As a maritime branch of the military, the United States Coast Guard has utilized a number of types of flags since the service was first organized by Alexander Hamilton on August 4, 1790. The United States Coast Guard even has its own version of a maritime ensign. **The United States Coast Guard Flag** is its formal land based flag.

 **98 The Flag of the United States Merchant Marine** honors an important branch of the United States Military that dates its service at least to June 12, 1775 and the American Revolution. Merchant mariners are non-uniformed civilian auxiliaries to the United States Navy in time of war, and are considered veterans entitled to veterans benefits if they have served during a conflict involving the United States. In World War II, the United States Merchant Marine sustained the highest percentage loss of life of any branch of the military.

American Veterans Flags

 99 On August 10, 1990, the United States Congress passed a resolution recognizing **The POW/MIA Flag** "as a symbol of our Nation's concern and commitment to resolving as fully as possible the fates of Americans still prisoner, missing and unaccounted for in Southeast Asia, thus ending the uncertainty for their families and the Nation." Subsequently, the flag has been recognized as a symbol for POW/MIAs from all U.S. wars.

 100 In 2006, a national campaign was begun in America for the adoption of a new flag honoring the battlefield dead of the United States in all wars, named **The Honor & Remember Flag**. The campaign's goal is stated as follows: "*To create, establish and promote a nationally recognized flag that would fly continuously as a visible reminder to all Americans of the lives lost in defense of our national freedoms. All Military lives lost not only in action but also in service, from our nation's inception.*"

Appendix
of
American Service Banners

   In 1917, United States Army Captain Robert L. Queisser created a service recognition flag to display in or outside of an American family's home with a Blue Star for every family member serving in a war at the time of display. **The Service Banner** became popular in World War I, and was extensively displayed in World War II, becoming popular again in the late 20th and early 21st Centuries. A gold star displayed on the Service Banner indicates a death of a family member in the military service, which may or may not have been battlefield related. On April 21, 2010, the United States House of Representatives officially recognized a "Silver Star Service Flag" in honor of those members of the military injured or falling ill and repatriated home.